Lakeland Cookery

compiled from recipes supplied by readers of Cumbria

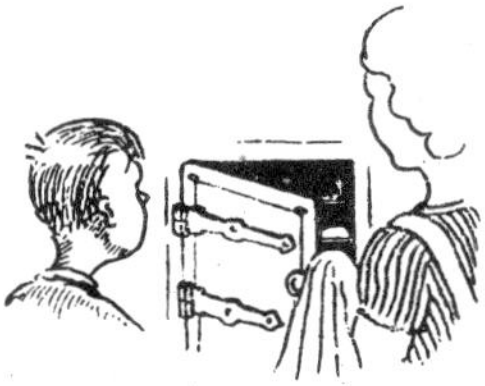

DALESMAN BOOKS
1973

The Dalesman Publishing Company Ltd.
Clapham (via Lancaster), Yorkshire

First Published 1969
Second edition 1971
Reprinted 1973

ISBN: 85206 069 6

*Printed in Great Britain by Galava Printing Co. Ltd.,
Hallam Road, Nelson, Lancs.*

LAKELAND COOKERY

30p

Contents

Cover illustration by E. JEFFREY

1. Traditional Recipes

CUMBERLAND SWEET PIE

Ingredients

½lb fat mutton chops (raw)
½lb currants
½lb sultanas
½lb raisins
6oz brown sugar
juice of one large lemon
a pinch each of cinnamon, mace, nutmeg, pepper
¼ teaspoon of salt
2oz mixed peel

Method. Fill pie dish with alternate layers of the mixture, beginning with mutton. Cover with rough puff pastry. Bake in a quick oven.

CUMBERLAND CAKE

Ingredients

shortcrust pastry
3oz sugar, or to own taste
6oz mixed dried fruit, or quantity liked, to cover pie dish used
1oz butter
1 egg white

Method. Line a pie plate with pastry and fill it with mixed dried fruit, sugar and butter. Cover with pastry and bake in a hot oven until pastry is golden. Spread with stiffly beaten egg white, sprinkle with sugar and return to oven to crisp. This cake is delicious cut into slices and eaten hot.

CUMBERLAND NICKIES

Ingredients

½lb short pastry
3oz currants
1 tablespoon demerara sugar
½ teaspoon grated nutmeg
1oz butter
1 tablespoon rum

Method. Melt butter, add nutmeg and rum. Now add currants and sugar. Leave to steep for an hour. Roll pastry thinly, cut into rounds, stir currant mixture well. Spread a little on one round of pastry: cover with another, prick. Bake in a hot oven for ten to fifteen minutes.

CHRISTMAS BREAD

Ingredients

1¾lb flour
3oz lard
6oz sugar
4oz currants
8oz raisins
4oz sultanas
1 tablespoon black treacle
2oz mixed peel
2 eggs
1 teaspoon spice
1 teaspoon salt
1oz yeast

Method. Put the flour and salt into a warm bowl and stand by the fire to warm. Rub in the lard. Cream the yeast in a basin with a teaspoon of sugar. Beat the eggs well and add sufficient warm milk and water to make threequarters of a pint, including the eggs. Stir into the yeast and mix well. Make a well in the middle of the flour and pour mixture in. Set to rise half an hour in a warm place, then knead well and add all the fruit, sugar, etc., warmed. Mix well and leave to rise for two hours; then put into two loaf tins. Rise for twenty minutes more and bake for one hour fifteen minutes, in a moderate oven.

CHRISTMAS CAKE

Ingredients

¾lb butter
¾lb soft brown sugar
6 eggs
¾lb flour
1lb sultanas
2lb currants
½lb cherries
6oz ground almonds
a pinch of mixed spice, ginger and cinnamon
½lb mixed peel

Method. Beat butter and sugar to a cream. Add eggs, well beaten. Then add flour and lastly fruit. Put into a lined cake tin. Bake in a slow oven for four hours. When cold, pour over cake 2 tablespoons of rum.

EASTER-LEDGE PUDDING

Ingredients

Easter-ledges about 4in high
half as many young nettles
1 large onion
teacup barley
½ teaspoon salt

Method. Remove stem of Easter-ledges and chop well together with young nettles and onion, wash the barley and sprinkle this in among the greens, adding the salt. Put all together and tie up in a muslin bag and boil for one and a half to two hours. Before serving beat it up in a dish with one egg and some butter (or bacon dripping is excellent) and flavour well with salt and pepper.

HOT CROSS BUNS

Ingredients

1lb flour
a pinch of salt
¾oz yeast
2 tablespoons sugar
2oz margarine
2oz currants
1 level teaspoon cinnamon
1 level teaspoon mixed spice
1 egg
about ½ pint milk

Method. Sieve flour with salt and spices, rub in fat and add currants. Cream the yeast with a little sugar, add a little warm milk and pour in centre of flour, sprinkle lightly over with flour and leave for ten minutes. Mix to a stiff dough with the beaten egg, adding a little milk if required. Allow to rise until the mixture doubles itself in size, divide into twelve portions, mould into small buns, mark with a cross and place on a greased and floured tin. Allow to rise until half as large again. Bake in a hot oven about eight minutes. Melt a little sugar in a tablespoonful of milk and brush over the buns when baked.

SNOW PANCAKES

Ingredients

1 heaped tablespoon flour
3 tablespoons of milk
a pinch of salt

Method. Mix to a stiff batter. Add 1 tablespoon of fine powdery snow. Again mix. Fry in available fat and serve with jam or dried fruit. The above quantities are for one pancake. Given the right kind of snow (not the wet, heavy variety) the results should be good.

EASTER CAKE

Ingredients

6oz flour
4oz castor sugar
4oz butter or margarine
4oz sultanas
2oz mixed peel
1oz almonds
2 eggs
1 tablespoon milk
½ teaspoon baking powder
grated rind of half a lemon

Method. Beat butter and sugar to a cream, and then beat in eggs. Add sifted flour, fruit, peel and almonds (blanched and sliced). Fold in baking powder and lemon rind; add milk and beat well. Bake for one and a half hours in moderate oven after placing mixture in paper-lined tin. Leave cake for two days. Then ice as follows: Sieve 6oz icing sugar into a bowl, add 1 teaspoon of lemon juice, a few drops of green colouring, and enough water to form a thin paste. Spread this over cake, first fastening a paper round cake to prevent icing running down sides. Stand cake in a warm place to dry. Remove paper next day, decorate with little marzipan ducklings or other Easter novelties, make little marzipan nests, fill with tiny eggs from confectioners or make some from icing sugar coloured green. Surround cake with a frill of green tissue paper, cut finely at edges to represent grass.

FAIR CAKES

These cakes were made at Whitsuntide and Martinmas for the Hiring Fair at Ulverston.

Ingredients

- 1lb flour
- ¼lb butter
- ¼lb lard
- a pinch salt
- ½oz fresh yeast
- 1 dessertspoon sugar
- ½ cup warm water

Method. Rub fat into dry ingredients, make a well in the centre and put in the yeast with the half cup of warm water and bind together. Roll out very thin and cut into 4 to 5 inch squares. Place a tablespoonful of the following mixture on half the squares, damp the edges with water, cover with the remaining pastry squares and pinch together round the edges.

Filling Mixture

- 1lb currants
- ½lb soft brown sugar
- 2oz candied peel, finely chopped
- a pinch of nutmeg
- a pinch of all-spice
- 1 teaspoonful rum

Mix all together and make a little softer with water or cold tea. Bake in hot oven until golden brown.

HERB PUDDING
(Oven method)

Method. Gather any greens available — Easter magiants (bistort), nettles, dandelion leaves, a few black currant leaves, onion, leek, a bit of cabbage or curly kale. Wash and dry in a cloth, chop up finely and place in a pie dish with a handful of oatmeal and one of barley. Salt and pepper to taste. Cover with water and leave overnight for meal and barley to swell. Cook as it is — the same time as cooking a roasting joint, about 1½ hours or more. Stir occasionally to keep from sticking to the dish.. If dish is greased first it doesn't stick so much. Just before serving, add a beaten egg and place in the oven for a few more minutes.

PENRITH SPICED PEPPER
(as bought from the shop of the late Tom Smith)

Ingredients

- 2oz white pepper
- 2oz ground nutmeg
- 2oz ground mace
- 1oz cayenne

Method. Mix all together, and keep in a well-corked bottle. Use the pepper as a flavouring for stews or any made-up meat dishes.

CLIPPING-TIME PUDDING

Ingredients

8oz rice
4oz currants
4oz stoned raisins
3oz sugar
1 egg
1 pint milk
a little cinnamon
2 beef marrow bones, cooked and marrow extracted
a little salt

Method. Blanch the rice in a little salt water, then cool it slowly in milk. Add sugar and cinnamon and boil until tender. Beat the egg and add to the rice, together with the currants and raisins, and stir well together. Then add the marrow, cut into small pieces. Bake for twenty minutes in a moderate oven (Regulo 7).

HAYMAKERS' COCKTAIL
(Westmorland)

Ingredients

½ pint orange juice from very sweet oranges
½ pint milk (new)

Method. Pour the orange juice slowly on to the milk, beating it into the milk all the time to ensure a thorough mixing. NO sugar should be added. The orange greatly increases the digestibility and palatability of the milk, making the drink refreshing and at the same time sustaining.

WESTMORLAND CREAM PANCAKES

Method. Mix 8oz flour, 1 level teaspoon carbonate of soda, 1 level teaspoon cream of tartar, pinch of salt, ¼ pint of cream. Mix with ¼ pint of milk (sour milk if possible), then the cream of tartar may be omitted. Dissolve bi-carbonate of soda and cream of tartar in the milk and cream mixture before adding to the flour and salt. Cook in lightly greased pan over moderate heat, turning when cooked on one side. This makes several pancakes of average size or you can make a larger number of small ones.

WESTMORLAND PEPPER CAKE

Ingredients

2lb flour
1lb sugar
1lb treacle
½lb butter
½lb currants
2oz candied lemon peel
½lb Valencia raisins
½oz clove pepper
1oz ginger
½ teaspoon black pepper
2 teaspoons baking powder
3 eggs

Method. Rub butter into flour, add fruit and spices, mix with treacle and eggs. Put into a well-greased cake tin and bake in a slow oven about three hours.

WESTMORLAND DAMSON PICKLE

Ingredients

6qts damsons (1½lb—1qt)
6lb sugar
1 quart vinegar
½oz whole cloves
¼oz ground cinnamon

Method. Choose firm, ripe damsons. Prick each one with a fork and put into a large bowl. Boil sugar, spices and vinegar, and pour over the damsons. Leave overnight. Next day drain off liquid, reboil, and pour over damsons. Leave overnight again. Next day boil all together for 3 to 5 minutes, keeping fruit as whole as possible. Put into hot jars and seal. This is excellent with cold mutton.

WESTMORLAND DUFF

Ingredients

2 breakfast cups flour
1½ cups sugar
1 teaspoon baking powder
2 eggs
¼lb butter or margarine

Method. Mix ingredients together and form into buns on a greased baking sheet. Bake in a cool oven for half an hour and then in a hotter oven for a similar period.

OUTGATE SATURDAY SPECIAL PUDDING

Ingredients

4oz butter
4oz flour
2oz coconut
4oz sugar
½ teaspoon baking powder
2 eggs
a little milk

Method. Cream the butter and sugar together. Beat in the eggs. Mix flour and baking powder, and stir into the creamed mixture. Lastly, add the coconut and a little milk. Pour into a greased pie dish. Bake in a moderate oven for one and a half hours.

GRASMERE GINGERBREAD

(as sold in the old days at all cafes en route to Grasmere on Sports Day)

Ingredients

1lb flour
½lb butter (or margarine)
½lb soft brown sugar
2 teaspoons of ground ginger
1 teaspoon carbonate of soda

Method. Rub in all dry ingredients and place in oblong flat tin, previously greased. Bake in moderate oven ten to fifteen minutes. Cut while hot.

KENDAL GINGER CAKE

Ingredients

3oz flour
3oz cornflour or ground rice
4oz butter
2oz sugar
1 teaspoon ground ginger
$\frac{1}{4}$ teaspoon baking powder
yolk of one egg
1 tablespoon milk
1oz candied peel
or grated rind of half a lemon

Method. Mix the flour, cornflour and baking powder in a bowl. Rub in the butter thoroughly, and then add sugar, ground ginger and candied peel (cut finely). Mix well together and make into a stiff paste with yolk and milk (beaten together). Roll out about a quarter of an inch thick and cut into fingers. Place on a baking tin and bake in a moderately quick oven about ten minutes, until slightly brown. When cold cover with a little icing or put together with jam between and ice over.

WINDERMERE SPICE BISCUITS

Ingredients

$\frac{1}{4}$lb butter
$\frac{1}{4}$lb sugar
1 teaspoon caraway seeds
6oz flour
$\frac{1}{2}$ teaspoon cinnamon
1 large egg

Method. Beat butter and sugar to a cream. Add the flour, caraway seeds and enough of the beaten egg to make a stiff paste. Roll out in rounds with a pastry cutter and bake for thirty minutes in a moderate oven.

BUTTERMERE BISCUITS

Ingredients

$\frac{1}{2}$lb flour
$\frac{1}{4}$lb butter
$\frac{1}{4}$lb castor sugar
a little grated lemon rind
$\frac{1}{2}$ teaspoon of baking powder
1 large egg
$1\frac{1}{2}$oz currants

Method. Rub the butter into the flour and add the sugar, lemon rind, currants and baking powder. Moisten with the beaten egg. Roll out a quarter of an inch thick. Cut into fancy shapes. Place on a greased tin and bake in a moderate oven for about twenty minutes.

—Thomas Parker

Early Morning in Troutbeck

2. Breads and Scones

WHOLEMEAL BREAD

Ingredients

3lb wholemeal flour
1 teaspoon brown sugar (or treacle)
2oz fresh yeast
1 tablespoon salt
$1\frac{1}{2}$ pints warm water (not hot)

Method. Mix salt and flour. Mix the yeast with the sugar or treacle in a little of the warm water and leave for about ten minutes to froth, then add to the flour, add the rest of the water and mix well by hand for several minutes until the dough leaves the sides of the mixing bowl clean, adding a little more flour if necessary. Put into loaf tins which have been greased and warmed, cover with a cloth and leave to rise until almost to the top of the tins. Bake in a hot oven about 40 minutes. Makes four, one pound loaves.

PLANT POT BREAD

Ingredients

$\frac{1}{2}$lb wholemeal flour
1oz fresh yeast
2 teaspoons salt
$\frac{1}{2}$lb white flour
1 teaspoon sugar
slightly less than $\frac{1}{2}$ pint warm water

This quantity is sufficient for a plant pot with a 5 inch diameter at the top. It is essential when first using a plant pot to bake bread that it should be well-greased and baked empty for about half an hour two or three times.

Method. Rub the yeast into the flour, salt and sugar, add the water and knead to a dough, adding a little more flour if necessary until the dough leaves the side of the bowl clean. Half fill a well-greased plant pot with the dough and allow to rise until double in size. Bake in a hot oven 30 to 40 minutes. This makes a delicious, crusty bread of good texture, as the plant pot retains the heat as did the old kiln ovens.

STICKY BREAD

Ingredients

2 teacups self-raising flour
4oz raisins
1 level teaspoonful bi-carb. soda
2 tablespoons sugar
2 tablespoons syrup
1 cup of milk and water

Method. Warm the syrup, dissolve bi-carb. soda in the milk and water and add to the warm syrup. Mix the dry ingredients and stir in the liquid ingredients. When well-blended place in a greased loaf tin and bake in a slow oven for about an hour.

NUT BREAD

Ingredients

½lb self-raising flour
1 egg
a little milk
3oz margarine
2oz walnuts

Method. Rub fat into flour. Add chopped nuts and beaten egg and milk, and make into a stiff dough. Put in greased tin and bake for half an hour in a moderate oven.

FRUIT LOAF (no eggs or fat)

Ingredients

4oz flour
4oz wholemeal flour, or 8oz of either
2oz sugar
3oz raisins
2oz chopped peel
1 teaspoon baking soda
½ gill milk
2 dessertspoons treacle
3oz currants
pinch salt
2 dessertspoons vinegar

Method. Mix all the dry ingredients and add milk. Add treacle and mix well, add the vinegar last. Turn into greased tin and bake in a moderate oven for our hour.

HONEY TWISTS

Ingredients

½oz yeast
1 tablespoon lukewarm water
¼pt milk
2oz margarine
1½oz sugar
1 egg yolk
12oz plain flour
1 level teaspoon salt
1oz chopped mixed candied peel
2oz sultanas

For the topping:

2oz margarine
1½oz sugar
3 level tablespoons honey
1 egg white

Method. Whisk yeast in lukewarm water. Heat the milk almost to boiling and pour over the margarine, sugar and salt in a bowl; allow to cool to lukewarm. Beat the egg yolk and whisk in, then add the flour, sultanas and chopped peel and beat well. Knead lightly and put in a warm place until the mixture doubles in size. Cream the margarine and sugar until fluffy, beat in the honey then add the unbeaten egg white and beat all until creamy and smooth. Knead the dough when proved. Roll out into a long piece an inch wide and coil into a previously greased 10 inch sandwich tin, beginning at the outer edge. Pour honey mixture over the dough. Allow to rise again until about double in size and bake in a moderate oven 15 to 20 minutes. Reduce heat to fairly moderate and continue to bake another 10 to 15 minutes.

COCONUT TWIST

Ingredients

1lb plain flour
3oz desiccated coconut and 1oz sugar or 4oz sweetened coconut
2 level teaspoons salt

Yeast Liquid: Blend ½oz fresh yeast in ½ pint milk and water mixed in which 1 teaspoon sugar has been dissolved *or* dissolve 1 teaspoon sugar in ½ pint warm milk and water mixed, 110° F., and sprinkle 2 level (standard) teaspoons dried yeast on top. Leave till frothy, about 10 minutes.

Method. Mix flour and salt, coconut and sugar in a bowl. Add yeast liquid and mix to a firm dough, adding more flour if necessary. Turn on to a lightly floured board and knead until the dough feels smooth and elastic. Place the dough in a greased polythene bag, lightly tied, plastic storage jar or saucepan with lid, and put to rise to double size, or until the dough springs back when pressed with a floured finger.

Choose rising times to suit your convenience:

45 to 60 minutes in a warm place.
2 hours at room temperature.
12 hours in a cold room or larder.
24 hours in a refrigerator.

When risen turn the dough on to a board lightly dusted with flour and coconut and knead. Divide the dough into three even pieces.

To shape: Roll the dough pieces out into three long strips and plait together. Form into a circle on a greased and floured baking sheet. Put inside a greased polythene bag to rise to double size. To keep a good shape this recipe is best risen slowly in a cold place.

Remove bag and bake on the middle shelf of a hot oven for 40 to 45 minutes or until golden brown. While still warm glaze with a wet brush dipped in honey or treacle. Cool on a wire tray.

When cold decorate with soft lemon icing and sprinkle with toasted coconut or flaked, toasted split almonds.

—T Parker.

Evening Sunlight by Ullswater

GRANDMA'S BUNLOAF

Ingredients

- 1lb plain flour
- 1lb currants
- ½lb sugar
- water to mix
- ½lb lard
- ½lb candied peel
- 1½ teaspoons bi-carbonate of soda

Method. Rub lard into flour, add sugar and fruit. Dissolve the bi-carbonate of soda in a little hot water and cool by adding a little cold water, mix into dry ingredients and use further cold water until mixture drops off the spoon. Line a greased tin with two layers of greaseproof paper. Pour in the mixture and bake in a moderate oven, about 2 hours.

HARVEST RING

Ingredients

Yeast Liquid:
- ¾oz fresh yeast or 1½ teaspoons dried yeast
- 6 tablespoons warm milk and water mixed
- 1 teaspoon sugar

Pastry:
- 8oz plain flour
- ½ level teaspoon salt
- 1 tablespoon sugar
- 1 egg
- 3oz margarine

Filling:
- 1oz butter
- 1oz icing sugar
- 6 drops vanilla flavouring

Decoration:
- water icing
- chopped almonds
- chocolate chips or candied cherries

Method. Dissolve sugar in warm milk and water. Blend in fresh yeast or sprinkle dried yeast on top. Leave in a warm place for about 10 minutes until frothy.

Mix flour, salt and sugar in a bowl, add egg and yeast liquid. Work to a firm dough. Turn on to a lightly-floured board and knead until smooth. Roll dough into strip 18in. x 6in. Cut the margarine into thin slices and spread a third over half the dough. Fold over the other half and seal edges with rolling pin. Roll into an 18in. x 6in. rectangle again, fold into three and seal edges. Turn round 90°. Repeat again with remaining two-thirds of margarine. Finally roll a strip 24in. x 4in. Cool pastry in the refrigerator or cool larder if it becomes too soft or sticky.

Cream filling ingredients and spread over the pastry. Roll up lengthwise and form into ring. Place on lightly greased and floured baking sheet. Snip deeply round top of ring with scissors, brush with beaten egg and put to rise slowly at room temperature, covered with a lightly oiled polythene bag until soft and springy—time depends on temperature.

Bake on the middle shelf of a moderately hot oven for about 15 to 20 minutes.

When cool, decorate with water icing and chopped almonds.

GINGER SCONES

Ingredients

- 8oz plain flour
- 1oz margarine
- 1oz castor sugar
- 2 level tablespoons syrup
- 1 egg
- 1 level teaspoon cream of tartar
- pinch salt
- 2 level teaspoons ground ginger
- 1 level teaspoon bi-carb. soda

Method. Rub fat into sieved flour. Add all other dry ingredients. Warm syrup and add. Mix to a soft dough with egg. Turn onto a floured board. Roll out and cut into small rounds. Put onto a greased tin and brush over with egg or milk. Bake in a hot oven 10 to 15 minutes.

LONSDALE SCONES

Ingredients

- 12oz plain flour
- 1 tablespoon sugar
- 1 teaspoon bi-carbonate soda
- 3½oz lard
- 2 teaspoons cream of tartar
- milk to make a soft dough

Method. Sift flour, cream of tartar and bi-carbonate soda into a bowl, rub in lard and mix in sugar. Make into a soft dough with milk. Roll out into rounds about ½ inch thick and bake in a hot oven about 15 minutes. These scones will keep fresh and soft for days in an airtight tin.

CRUNCHY TOP YEAST CAKE

Ingredients

- 8oz plain flour
- 2oz sugar
- 1oz fresh yeast or 1 level tablespoon dried yeast (½oz)
- ⅛ pint milk (5 tablespoons)
- 2 to 3 tablespoons jam
- 2oz fine semolina
- 3oz margarine
- grated rind of an orange
- 2 eggs
- 2oz currants

Topping

- 2oz butter or margarine
- 2oz sugar
- 2oz plain flour
- 2 rounded teaspoons cinnamon

Method. Sieve or mix dry ingredients into a basin. Rub in fat followed by yeast (if using dried yeast see note below). Add beaten eggs and milk, using a wooden spoon, to make a soft dough. Mix in orange rind and currants. Turn into a greased and floured shallow baking tin, 8½" x 5½", and spread evenly with wet fingers. Spread jam thinly over top of cake. Rub topping ingredients lightly together to form a crumble and sprinkle over jam. Put to rise to double in size in a warm place (about 30 minutes). Bake in a fairly hot oven near the top, for 30 to 40 minutes. Turn out and cool on a wire tray.

Delicious served buttered when very fresh, or toasted.

CHEESE SCONES

Ingredients

1lb self-raising flour
1 teaspoon dry mustard
8oz grated cheese
½ teaspoon salt
2oz margarine
½ pint milk

Method. Sift together flour, salt and mustard. Rub in margarine until mixture resembles fine breadcrumbs. Add 7oz grated cheese and bind together with milk to form a soft dough. Roll out on a floured board to ½ inch thickness and cut into rounds with a 1½ inch plain cutter. Place on greased baking sheets, brush with milk and sprinkle remaining grated cheese on top. Bake in a hot oven for about 12 minutes.

TREACLE SCONES

Ingredients

1lb plain flour
½ teaspoon cream of tartar
1 teaspoon mixed spice
2oz butter or margarine
2 tablespoons black treacle
1 teaspoon bi-carb. soda
1 teaspoon ground cinnamon
½ teaspoon salt
2 teaspoons sugar
½ pint milk

Method. Sift together all dry ingredients, except sugar. Rub in butter until mixture resembles fine breadcrumbs, then add sugar and treacle. Mix to a soft dough with milk. Turn out on a lightly floured board, knead lightly then roll out to ½in thickness. Cut into 3in. triangles and brush tops with milk. Place on a greased baking sheet. Bake in a hot oven for about 15 minutes. Serve fresh from the oven while still warm with butter.

FRUIT GIRDLE SCONES

Ingredients

½lb plain flour
1 level teaspoon cream of tartar
pinch of salt
1oz sultanas
2oz margarine
fat for greasing girdle or hotplate
½ level teaspoon bi-carb. soda
1oz castor sugar
2oz currants
about ¼ pint of milk

Method. Sieve dry ingredients and rub in margarine. Add fruit. Add milk and mix with knife to a stiff dough. Roll out on floured board about ¼ inch thick. Cut into small rounds and bake on hot greased girdle or hotplate, turning once, until brown on both sides.

3. Cakes and Biscuits

OLD FASHIONED PARKIN

Ingredients

- ¼lb plain flour
- ¾teaspoon bi-carb. soda
- ½lb medium oatmeal
- ½lb brown sugar
- 1 egg
- ½ teaspoon cinnamon
- 1 heaped teaspoon ground ginger
- ½lb black treacle
- 3oz butter or margarine
- 5 to 6 tablespoons milk

Method. Sieve together the flour, cinnamon, ginger and bi-carbonate of soda and add the oatmeal. Slowly melt the butter or margarine, treacle and sugar in a saucepan and add, with the beaten egg, to the flour mixture. Lastly stir in the milk and mix thoroughly to form a fairly soft batter. Turn into a square tin lined with greased greaseproof paper and bake in a slow oven, 40 to 50 minutes. Cut, the following day, into thick fingers or squares.

CUMBERLAND SODA CAKE

Ingredients

- 1lb flour
- ½lb sugar
- ½lb currants
- 2 teaspoons bi-carb. soda
- ½lb sultanas
- ½lb margarine
- 1oz candied peel
- pinch salt

Method. Rub fat in flour and mix rest of ingredients, except bi-carbonate of soda. Dissolve in 2 tablespoonsful of milk and mix all together. Stand overnight. Put into a greased cake tin. Bake in a slow oven next morning for two hours.

CUMBERLAND PASTRY CAKE

Ingredients

Pastry:

- 1lb flour
- ½lb lard
- 2oz butter
- a little salt and cold water to mix

Filling:

- 1lb currants
- 1oz butter
- 4oz castor sugar
- 1oz finely shredded peel
- pinch of spice and teaspoonful of rum

Method. Make pastry and divide into two, and roll each piece ¼ inch thick. Put currants into a saucepan with butter, sugar, peel, spice and rum. Heat up then turn into a basin to cool. When cold, spread the mixture evenly on one piece of pastry, cover with other piece. Press edges together, prick top and bake about 30 mins. in a good oven. Sift castor sugar over top when cold.

CUMBERLAND ELDERBERRY CAKE

Ingredients

elderberries; sugar	½lb short crust pastry

Method. Roll out the pastry and line a pie plate. Fill with elderberries and sugar to taste, cover with pastry and bake in a hot oven. When cool spread with a very thin layer of white icing.

GINGERBREAD

Ingredients

1lb flour	½lb treacle
½lb syrup	½lb brown sugar
½lb lard or margarine	3 eggs
¼ pint milk	¼teaspoon salt
¼ teaspoon mixed spice	1 dessertspoon ground ginger
½ teaspoon bi-carb. soda	a little chopped candied peel (optional)

Method. Warm milk and dissolve lard in it, add treacle, syrup and beaten eggs. Add to the dry ingredients which have been previously blended and mix all well together. Put into a shallow, well-greased tin. Bake in a moderate oven for one hour.

RICH WINDERMERE FRUIT CAKE

Ingredients

- 8oz flour, plain or self-raising
- ½ teaspoon spice
- 6oz soft brown sugar
- 8oz currants
- 2oz chopped candied peel
- 2oz blanched chopped almonds
- ¼ teaspoon salt
- 6oz butter
- 4 eggs
- 6oz sultanas
- 2oz glace cherries

Method. Beat margarine and sugar until light and fluffy. Add the beaten eggs, one at a time, then gradually add the flour and fruit. Place in a tin lined with greased paper and bake in a moderate oven for half-an-hour, then reduce the oven to slow and bake a further two hours or until the cake remains firm when lightly pressed with a knife.

BLACKBERRY CREAM CAKE

Ingredients

- 4oz margarine
- 2 beaten eggs
- 4oz castor sugar
- 4oz self-raising flour

Filling:

- ½ pint double cream
- 1oz castor sugar
- 8oz blackberries

Method. Cream margarine and sugar until mixture is light and fluffy. Gradually beat in egg, adding a little flour with last addition of egg. Fold in remaining flour. Divide mixture between two greased 7 inch sandwich tins and bake in a moderate oven for 20 minutes. Turn out and leave to cool.

Whisk cream until stiff. Spread one of the sponges with half the cream. Remove centre of other sponge with a 3½ inch biscuit cutter and keep on one side. Sandwich sponges together. Wash blackberries and sprinkle with sugar. Pile into centre of cake, keeping 6 for decoration. Cut remaining centre of sponge into 6 wedges and arrange around blackberries with points facing outwards. Spoon a teaspoon of cream between each and top with a blackberry.

HAWKSHEAD CAKE

Ingredients

- 1¾lb flour
- 3oz yeast
- 4oz sultanas
- ½lb soft brown sugar
- 1½ level teaspoons baking powder
- ¾lb margarine
- 1lb currants
- 2oz candied peel
- pinch of salt
- about ¾ pint warm (not hot) milk

Method. Rub in the yeast, dry. Mix together the flour, sugar and salt. Rub in the fat, mix in the fruit, then mix with the warm milk. Put into well-greased tins and allow to rise in a warm place for half an hour before baking in a moderate oven about 30 to 40 minutes.

HAWKSHEAD BISCUITS

Ingredients

1lb self-raising flour	3oz butter
1oz castor sugar	a pinch salt
1 egg, well-beaten	½ pint milk

Method. Rub the butter into the flour, add the sugar and salt and mix to a light dough with the beaten egg and milk. Divide into eight pieces, roll each piece out about ½ inch thick, prick all over with a fork, place on greased baking sheets and bake in a moderate oven about 15 minutes.

COCONUT SHORTBREAD

Ingredients

1 cup self-raising flour	½ cup castor sugar
2oz butter	1 egg yolk

Method. Rub butter into flour, add sugar and mix, add egg yolk and knead together. Press into greased swiss-roll tin and spread with a layer of raspberry jam.

Topping: 1½ cups coconut, ½ cup castor sugar, well-beaten white of one egg. Mix well together and spread on top of the shortbread Bake in a moderate oven about 20 minutes or until golden brown. Cut into fingers when almost cold.

ULVERSTON SHORTBREAD OR MEG'S SHORTBREAD

Ingredients

2oz icing sugar	4oz margarine
6oz self-raising flour	

Method. Blend the icing sugar and flour, rub in the fat to form a dough (no liquid should be used). Roll out about ½ inch thick, cut into rounds and place in a greased baking sheet. Bake in a moderate oven until golden brown.

CHOCOLATE SHORTCAKE

Ingredients

1 cup flour	1 cup coconut
4oz margarine	1 tablespoon cocoa

Method. Mix the dry ingredients, rub in the fat until the mixture is crumbly. Press into a well-greased, oblong tin and bake in a moderate oven about 20 minutes. When baked make a chocolate icing and spread over the shortbread while still hot.

GINGER BISCUITS

Ingredients

- 8oz self-raising flour
- 3oz margarine
- 1 level teaspoon ground ginger.
- 4oz sugar
- 1 large tablespoon treacle

Method. Warm the treacle. Mix flour, ginger and sugar, rub in fat, mix in the treacle and knead. Place small balls of the mixture on greased baking sheets and flatten with a fork. Bake in a moderate oven 10 to 15 minutes.

ALMOND BISCUITS

Ingredients

- 3oz plain flour
- 4oz ground almonds
- 1 egg
- a few glace cherries
- 3oz castor sugar
- 2oz margarine
- 1 teaspoon almond essence

Method. Rub margarine into flour, add sugar, ground almonds and mix well together. Beat the egg and add to the mixture along with the almond essence. Mix to a soft paste. Mould with the hands into small flat biscuits, place half a glace cherry on top of each. Put on a greased baking sheet and bake in a moderate oven 20 to 30 minutes.

DATE AND WALNUT SLICES

Ingredients

- 1 cup self-raising flour
- 1 cup chopped dates
- 4oz margarine or butter
- 1 cup chopped walnuts
- 1 cup soft brown sugar
- 2 eggs

Method. Melt the margarine and sugar together, mix in the flour, walnuts and dates, beat the eggs and add to the mixture gradually. Put into a greased swiss-roll tin and bake in a moderate oven about 20 minutes.

COCONUT SHORTBREAD

Ingredients

- 2 cups self-raising flour
- 1 cup sugar
- 1 cup coconut
- ½lb margarine

Method. Mix together the dry ingredients, rub in the margarine, knead well, roll out quite thinly and cut into shapes. Place on greased baking sheets and bake in a moderate oven about 10 minutes until turning golden brown.

OATY PARKINS

Ingredients

- 1 cup flour
- 2 cups oats
- 1 tablespoon treacle
- pinch salt
- 1 cup sugar
- ¼lb margarine and lard mixed
- 1 level teaspoon bi-carb. soda
- 1 level teaspoon ginger

Method. Heat treacle and fat together, mix bi-carb. soda with a little hot water and stir into the treacle and fat, add dry ingredients and mix, adding a little more water if necessary, but do not make too soft. Roll out on a floured board, cut into rounds with a biscuit cutter and bake in a moderate oven, 10 to 15 minutes.

BUTTERSCOTCH STRIPS

Ingredients

- 2 cups oats
- ½ cup butter or margarine
- 1 teaspoon vanilla essence
- 1 cup soft brown sugar
- ½ level teaspoon bi-carb. soda

Method. Melt sugar and fat in a pan but do not allow to boil, add the bi-carb. soda and mix well in. Remove from heat and stir in oats and vanilla essence. Press the mixture into a well greased swiss-roll tin and bake in a slow oven, 10 to 15 minutes. Cut into strips when still warm.

GINGER DROPS

Ingredients

- 3oz margarine
- 6oz flour
- 1 tablespoon syrup
- ½ teaspoon bi-carb. soda
- 3oz soft brown sugar
- 1oz oatmeal or oats
- ½ teaspoon ginger

Method. Cream sugar and margarine, add syrup and beat well. Add sifted flour, ginger and soda, then the oatmeal or oats. Roll into balls about the size of a walnut, place on a greased baking sheet, and bake in a moderate oven about 15 minutes.

GINGER SNAPS

Ingredients

- 12oz self-raising flour
- 4oz margarine
- 2 heaped teaspoons ginger
- ¼ teaspoon salt
- 1 egg
- 8oz sugar
- 4oz syrup
- 1 heaped teaspoon bi-carb. soda

Method. Melt margarine and syrup in a pan. Mix all dry ingredients together. Add melted margarine and syrup and beaten egg. Mix to a stiff consistency and shape into pieces the size of a walnut, put on a greased baking sheet and bake in a moderate oven, 15 to 20 minutes.

COCONUT BISCUITS

Ingredients

- 3oz sugar
- 3oz coconut
- 1 large tablespoon syrup
- pinch of salt
- 3oz margarine
- 4oz plain flour
- ½ teaspoon bi-carb. soda

Method. Cream sugar, margarine and syrup together, then add other ingredients and mix well. Place on a greased baking sheet in little balls. Bake in a moderate oven until golden brown.

GRASMERE GINGERBREAD CAKE

Ingredients

- 4oz butter
- 3 eggs
- 1 teaspoon baking powder
- 3oz preserved ginger
- a little grated lemon rind
- 4oz sugar
- 10oz plain flour
- ¼ teaspoon ground ginger
- 1 tablespoon syrup from preserved ginger

Method. Beat the butter and sugar to a cream, add each egg separately and beat thoroughly. Stir in flour, baking powder and ground ginger. Cut preserved ginger into small squares and add to the mixture with the syrup and lemon rind. Pour into tin lined with greased paper. Bake 1¾ hours in a slow oven.

CHOCOLATE CAKE

Ingredients

- 3oz self-raising flour
- 2oz margarine
- 1 egg
- 1 egg-cupful boiling water
- 4oz sugar
- 1oz cocoa
- 3 tablespoons milk

Method. Cream margarine and sugar, beat in egg, mix flour and cocoa and sieve into mixture. Add milk and beat until smooth. Stir in boiling water and put into a well-greased cake tin. Bake in a slow oven about 45 minutes.

COFFEE AND CINNAMON CAKES

Ingredients

- 8oz plain flour
- 1oz castor sugar
- 2½oz butter or margarine
- 2 level teaspoons baking powder
- milk to mix, flavoured well with coffee

Filling:

- Castor sugar as required
- 1½oz butter or margarine
- coffee syrup
- 1 level teaspoon cinnamon
- 2oz sultanas

Method. Sieve flour and baking powder and mix in sugar. Rub in fat finely, then mix to a soft but not sticky dough with the coffee-flavoured milk. Knead lightly for a moment to make smooth, then roll out about ¼ inch thick to an oblong about 10 inches by 8 inches. Brush a little coffee syrup over surface of dough — sparingly. Then sprinkle with castor sugar, mixed with cinnamon. Melt fat without oiling and brush over dough within an inch of the edges. Sprinkle with sultanas. Moisten edges of dough then roll up and seal firmly along join. Wrap in waxed or greaseproof paper and chill in refrigerator. Cut into ¾ inch wide slices with a sharp knife and bake lying flat on a greased baking tin in a brisk oven Mark 7 (420°F.) until cakes are risen and golden brown. Dust with powdered sugar before serving.

NUTTY DAINTIES

Ingredients

4oz butter or margarine
4oz rolled oats
1½ tablespoons syrup
4oz sugar
4oz desiccated coconut

Method. Mix all dry ingredients together, melt butter and syrup and when cool add. Place in shallow, greased tins and bake in a slow oven. Cut into fingers when cooling.

LEMON BUNS

Ingredients

1lb plain flour
pinch of salt
2oz margarine
lemon essence
½ pint warm milk.
1oz yeast
2oz sugar
2oz sultanas
1 egg

Method. Put flour into large bowl, add salt and rub in the margarine. Make a hole in the centre and add sugar, yeast and a few drops of lemon essence. Beat up the egg and add warm milk to it. Then pour it into the centre to mix up the yeast until it is a creamy substance. Set in a warm place for 15 minutes and then work all the flour into it until you get a soft dough. Set to "rise" again for 30 minutes, then cut into small pieces and work into bun shapes. Allow to rise on baking shelf until about twice their size, then bake in a hot oven for about 15 minutes. When cold cover with icing to which has been added a few drops of lemon essence.

4. Hot and Cold Puddings

APRICOT FLUFFY PIE

Ingredients

1 large tin of apricot halves, drained of syrup
4oz castor sugar
2 eggs
few drops vanilla essence
5oz self-raising flour, sifted
pinch of salt
4oz softened butter or margarine

Method. Put fruit into bottom of a well-greased ovenproof dish, approximately 8in. in diameter. Just cover with some of the fruit syrup. Place all cake ingredients into a bowl and beat until smooth and well blended, about 5 minutes. Spoon mixture on top of fruit. Bake in centre of a moderate oven for 30 to 35 minutes. Dust top with sieved icing sugar and serve hot with warmed apricot syrup from can and cream or ice cream.

FLUFFY FRUIT SHORTCAKE

Ingredients

8oz self-raising flour
4oz margarine
1 egg (beaten)
3oz sugar
pinch salt
5 tablespoons milk

Method. Mix the dry ingredients and rub in the fat. Mix egg and milk and add gradually to the flour mixture, making a very soft dough. Divide dough into two and press lightly into two well greased sandwich tins. Bake in a moderate oven for 20 minutes. When cold spread one cake with crushed raspberries or strawberries, place the other cake on top, cover top and sides with whipped cream, decorate with whole fruit.

PRUNE WHIP

Ingredients

3 egg whites
2 tablespoons lemon juice
1 cup chopped cooked prunes
1 tablespoon grated lemon peel
$\frac{1}{3}$ cup sugar

Method. Combine all ingredients except prunes in a double boiler over boiling water and whisk for ten minutes or until mixture holds its shape, fold in the prunes and serve with custard sauce or cream.

CUSTARD FRITTERS

Method. Beat up the yolks of 8 eggs with a tablespoon of flour, half a grated nutmeg, a pinch of salt and a glass of brandy; add a pint of cream, sweeten to taste and bake in a small dish. When cold cut into slices and dip these in a batter made as follows: mix half a pint of cream, quarter-pint of milk, 4 eggs, a little flour and a pinch of ground ginger. Fry them, and when done strew over with castor sugar.

COWSLIP PUDDING

Ingredients

- 1pt cowslip petals
- 2oz breadcrumbs
- 1 dessertspoon lemon juice
- ½ pt milk
- 2oz sugar
- yolks of three eggs

Method. Stew the cowslip petals in the milk until tender, then add other ingredients. Steam in a buttered mould for 1½ hours. Serve with white sauce or custard.

APPLE CORNFLOUR PUDDING

Ingredients

- ½ pint milk
- 3 teaspoons cream
- nutmeg
- 1lb cooking apples stewed and sweetened
- 1 to 2 eggs
- 2 dessertspoons cornflour blended with a little milk
- 4 oz sugar

Method. Put the milk in a saucepan, add the sugar. Stir in the blended cornflour and add the beaten eggs, cream and a little grated nutmeg. Pour half the mixture into a greased pie dish, spread with cooked apple and cover with the rest of the mixture. Bake in a moderately hot oven for 20 minutes.

GINGER PUDDING

Ingredients

- 3oz flour
- 3oz breadcrumbs
- 4oz preserved ginger
- little milk if required
- ½ teaspoon ground ginger
- 3oz chopped suet
- 3oz demerara sugar
- 3 eggs
- pinch of salt
- ½ teaspoon bi-carb. soda

Method. Dice the preserved ginger. Put all dry ingredients in a basin, mix in the diced ginger and beaten eggs and a little milk if necessary. Pour into a mould which has been thickly buttered and dusted with sugar, filling the basin three-parts full. Steam for 2 hours. Serve with a white sauce flavoured with ginger syrup and a little cut up ginger.

CONISTON PUDDING

Ingredients

- 6oz short crust pastry
- 1oz currants
- 1 egg
- 1 dessertspoon sugar
- 1oz raisins
- ½oz candied peel
- ¼ pint milk
- a little grated nutmeg

Method. Line a flat enamel dish with pastry and decorate the edges. Beat up the egg, add the sugar and nutmeg, then the milk (which should be hot). Chop the peel and raisins rather coarsely, add these with the currants to the custard and pour into the prepared dish. Bake in a moderate oven for 50 minutes.

RAISIN NUT PIE

Ingredients

- ½lb short crust pastry
- ½ cup sugar
- juice of half an orange
- ½ cup chopped walnuts
- 2 tablespoons cornflour
- 1 cup seedless raisins
- juice of half a lemon
- ¾ cup of boiling water
- ¼ teaspoon salt
- a little butter

Method. Cook raisins in boiling water for 5 minutes, mix sugar, cornflour and salt together and add to the raisins. Cook until thick, remove from heat, add lemon and orange juice, and when cold stir in the nuts. Line a pie plate with short crust pastry, fill with the mixture, dot with butter and cover with a lid of pastry. Brush over with water, sprinkle with sugar and bake in a hot oven for 10 minutes, then reduce heat to moderate and leave for a further 10 minutes.

DATE PUDDING

Ingredients

- ½lb stoned dates
- 2oz white bread crumbs
- 1 tablespoon treacle
- pinch salt
- 3oz self-raising flour
- 2oz shredded suet
- 1 egg
- milk to mix

Method. Mix suet, flour and breadcrumbs, chop the dates and add, mix well. Then add the treacle, egg (well-beaten) and milk to make a soft mixture. Put into a well greased basin, cover with greased greaseproof paper and steam for three hours.

GOOSEBERRY CHARLOTTE

Ingredients

- sponge cake
- ½ pint custard
- ½oz gelatine
- sugar to taste
- cooked, sieved gooseberries
- 1 teaspoon lemon juice

Method. Line a plain mould with fingers of sponge cake. Stew a generous lb of gooseberries with ½ pint of water and sweeten to taste. When tender run through a sieve and allow to cool. When quite cold stir in the custard to which the gelatine has been added. Next add the lemon juice, and pour the mixture into the prepared mould.

PINEAPPLE MERINGUES

Ingredients

2 peach halves
3 egg whites
6oz castor sugar
2 pieces of swiss-roll about 1 inch thick
angelica leaves

Method. Place peach halves on rounds of swiss-roll. Whisk egg whites until stiff, fold in the sugar. Put meringue mixture into a piping bag with a plain tube and pipe on to peach halves to represent a pineapple. Stick angelica leaves on top and place in a hot oven 10 to 15 minutes until golden brown.

CHOCOLATE MOUSSE

Ingredients

4 eggs
4oz plain chocolate
¼ pint double cream
walnuts

Method. Melt chocolate in a basin over hot water. Separate the eggs and add the yolks to the chocolate; mix in well. Whip egg whites until stiff and whip half the cream; add these to the chocolate and fold in gently. Whip the rest of the cream and decorate the mousse with this, finish off with walnuts.

CHARLOTTE SPECIAL

Ingredients

Pastry:

8oz flour
6oz butter
1 oz sugar
1 egg yolk
juice of half small lemon
1 tablespoon cold water

Method. Rub butter into sifted flour until mixture resembles fine breadcrumbs. Stir in sugar and mix in egg yolk, lemon juice and water. Wrap and chill for one hour.

Filling:

1½lb apples
4oz sugar
1 level teaspoon cinnamon
2oz raisins
2oz currants
grated rind of half a lemon

Method. Peel, core and slice apples and mix with the rest of ingredients. Divide pastry into two parts, one part being twice as big as the other. Roll out larger piece to line an 8 inch pie plate. Fill with apple mixture and top with the rest of the pastry rolled out to fit. Score top in diamond pattern, brush lightly with milk and sprinkle with a tablespoon of granulated sugar. Bake in centre of a hot oven for 20 minutes, then lower heat to medium for another 30 to 40 minutes.

BANANA DESSERT CAKE

Hot Cake for Dinner

Most dinners need to be good double features when the weather is cold. Hearty main course and then a satisfying pudding. This Banana Dessert cake is just that. It is also light and luscious and is served hot from the oven — or it can be made at any time during the day.

Ingredients

- 8oz plain flour
- 1 level teaspoon bi-carb. soda
- 4oz castor sugar
- 2 medium bananas, well mashed
- 2 tablespoons milk
- 1 tablespoon lemon juice
- large pinch salt
- 5oz butter or margarine
- 3 large eggs
- 1oz chopped walnuts (optional)

Method. Sift dry ingredients. Cream fat and sugar till light and fluffy, then beat in eggs, one at a time, adding a tablespoon of flour with each. Stir in bananas and nuts then gently fold in rest of flour alternately with the milk and lemon juice. Turn into a well greased 7 inch square cake tin, lined on the bottom with greaseproof paper. Bake in the centre of a moderate oven, 40 minutes or till cake is well risen and firm. Serve hot with cream or custard, and for an extra a garnish of walnuts.

HAZELNUT PEAR PIE

Ingredients

Pastry:

- 6oz plain flour
- 3oz butter
- 2 egg yolks blended with 1 tablespoon water
- $\frac{1}{4}$ level teaspoon salt
- 2oz castor sugar
- 3oz hazelnuts, finely ground

Filling:

- $\frac{3}{4}$lb firm dessert pears, peeled, cored and sliced
- 5oz carton single or double cream
- 2oz castor sugar
- 1 teaspoon lemon juice

Decoration:

double cream, whipped

Method.

Pastry: Sift together flour and salt. Rub in butter until mixture resembles fine breadcrumbs. Mix in sugar and ground nuts. Mix to form a soft dough with egg yolks and water. Chill for 10 minutes. Reserve one quarter of pastry for the lid, roll out remaining pastry and use to line an 8in. flan ring. Roll out pastry for lid into an 8in. circle and cut a 3in. circle out of centre.

Filling: Mix sliced pears with sugar and lemon juice and arrange in line flan ring. Pour over cream.

Dampen edges of pastry, place lid carefully over fruit and seal edges, trimming if necessary. Bake in a fairly hot oven for about 45 minutes until fruit is cooked and pastry golden.

Leave to cool. Pipe whipped cream into hole in centre of pie just before serving.

VANILLA AND APRICOT DINNER CAKE

Ingredients

6oz butter
3 drops vanilla essence
8oz self-raising flour, sifted
vanilla cream (see below)
almonds, blanched, split and toasted, for decoration
6oz castor sugar
3 medium eggs
3 tablespoons milk
1 large tin apricots

Method. Cream butter, sugar and vanilla together till light and fluffy. Beat in eggs, one at a time, adding a tablespoon of flour with each. Fold in rest of flour alternately with the milk then turn into a well greased 8in. ring tin. Bake in the centre of a fairly moderate oven about one hour. Turn out and cool on a wire tray.

Cut cake in half horizontally and sandwich together with a thick layer of vanilla cream and 4 to 5 apricot halves drained and coarsely chopped. Spread top and sides of filled cake with remaining vanilla cream then decorate top with the toasted almonds. Chill before serving and accompany with a bowl of apricot halves.

Vanilla Cream:

6oz butter or margarine
1 tablespoon milk
12oz icing sugar, sieved
4 drops vanilla essence and 2 drops of almond essence (no more)

Method. Cream butter and icing sugar together till light, fluffy and smooth. Beat in milk and essences.

PEACH SPICE CAKE

Ingredients

6oz self-raising flour
2 level teaspoons mixed spice
6oz butter or margarine
3 medium eggs
large pinch salt
1 level teaspoon cinnamon
6oz caster sugar

Vanilla Cream:

6oz butter or margarine
12oz icing sugar, sieved
1 teaspoon vanilla essence
2 tablespoons milk.

Beat fat and vanilla essence till soft then gradually stir in the sugar alternately with the milk. Cream well till mixture is light, fluffy and smooth.

Decoration:

6 peach halves, drained of syrup
1oz walnuts, finely chopped

Method. Sift together dry ingredients. Cream fat and sugar till light and fluffy then add eggs, one at a time, beating thoroughly after each addition. Fold in dry ingredients then divide mixture equally between two well greased 8 inch sandwich tins. Bake just above centre of a moderate oven, for 25 to 30 minutes. Turn out on to a wire tray and leave till cold.

Split each cake in half then sandwich layers together with vanilla cream. Spread remainder over top and sides of cake then press walnuts against the sides. Arrange peach halves on top then decorate with small teaspoons of vanilla cream. Chill before serving if possible.

BLACKBERRY AND APPLE PUDDING

Ingredients

1lb cooking apples	1lb blackberries
1 pint water	4oz sugar
9 to 12 slices fresh white bread	

Method. Peel and core apples and slice thinly. Simmer apples and blackberries in water until tender. Stir in sugar until dissolved. Cool.

Remove crusts from bread. Trim a circle of bread to fit bottom of a 2 pint pudding basin. Line sides of basin with fingers of bread, shaped wider at one end than the other, and fit well together. Add a little fruit and juice. Cover with a layer of bread. Continue until basin is full, finishing with a layer of bread, about 3 layers in all. Cover with a plate, which fits top of basin, and place a heavy weight on top.

Leave in a refrigerator or cool place overnight. Turn out and serve with cream.

5. Soups

GAME SOUP

Ingredients

- the remains of any cold game
- 2 medium sized carrots
- 1 bay leaf
- 2 peppercorns
- 2oz finely chopped liver
- 1 wine glass sherry to every quart of stock
- 1 large onion
- 1 bunch mixed herbs (quantity and mixture to taste)
- 2 or 3 cloves
- the whites of 2 eggs
- 1 teaspoonful brown sugar
- poultry stock or water

Method. Put the game into a pan with the chopped liver, onion, carrots, herbs, bay leaf, peppercorns, cloves and sugar. Cover with stock or water and bring to the boil. Simmer for one hour, then strain and when cold add the egg whites lightly beaten, and a wineglass of sherry to every quart of stock and whisk all well together. Put the game meat, cut into small pieces, back into the soup, thicken as desired, return to the pan and bring to the boil.

CELERY SOUP

Ingredients

- 1oz dripping
- 1lb celery
- a good pinch of grated nutmeg
- 1 pint stock or water
- 1 large onion
- ½ teaspoon sugar
- salt and pepper to season

Method. Put the vegetables, cut small, into a saucepan in whch you have melted the dripping, add sugar and nutmeg and season with salt and pepper, allow to cook gently for about 10 minutes, stirring to prevent burning. Add the pint of stock or water and simmer for about 1 hour, then add the thickening and cook for a further 10 minutes, stirring continuously. Sieve well, and add a little more salt and pepper if required.

Thickening: 1oz flour, 1oz dripping, ½ pint milk

Melt the dripping in a pan, stir in the flour, allow to cook for a few minutes, add the milk and cook until the mixture thickens, stirring all the time, then add to the soup and bring all to the boil.

VEGETABLE SOUP

Ingredients

2 shin bones
1 head of celery
2oz rice, macaroni or spaghetti
1 carrot
1 slice of turnip
salt and pepper

Method. Place bones in pan, cover well with water. Bring to boil and simmer for 2 to 3 hours. Strain, and if needed leave to go cold and take off fat. Add the cleaned vegetables, finely chopped, salt and pepper and rice, bring to the boil and simmer until all are tender.

MUTTON BROTH

Ingredients

1lb scrag end of mutton
4 teaspoons salt
½ teaspoon pepper
1 tablespoon rice
4 pints stock
1 tablespoon parsley
1 pint diced leek, onion, carrot

Method. Wipe the meat, remove skin, fat and gristle, and cut into small pieces. Put the meat, with any bones into a pan, add the salt, the required amount of stock, and the rice, bring to simmering point and cook at this temperature for two hours. Add the diced vegetables, and cook for one hour longer. Add the pepper and parsley, also extra salt and pepper if necessary and serve very hot.

CREAM OF POTATO SOUP

Ingredients

1 or 2 cups chopped cooked boiled or steamed potatoes
2 cups potato water
3 cups hot milk
salt and pepper to taste
1½oz butter
1½oz flour
1 small onion, chopped finely
1 teaspoon chopped parsley

Method. Place the potatoes in a saucepan. Add potato water and chopped onion and parsley. Cover and simmer for 20 minutes. Melt butter in another pan. Stir in flour, off the heat, and when smooth, stir in hot milk by degrees. Return to heat and stir till boiling. Add the potato broth which may be whisked or sieved. Season to taste with salt and pepper. Add parsley. Enough for 4 to 6 persons.
NOTE — Boiled and sieved turnip may be added if desired.

6. Meat Dishes and Savouries

NORTH COUNTRY STEAK

Ingredients

- 1lb stewing steak, cut about 1½ inches thick
- 1 medium sized onion, finely chopped
- 3 bay leaves
- 2 teapoons finely chopped parsley
- 2oz butter
- 1 pint beef stock
- salt and pepper to season

Method. Mix the chopped parsley and onion. Score the steak with a sharp kinfe and rub the chopped parsley and onion into the cuts. Leave for an hour, season with salt and pepper and fry in the butter until well browned. Put into a casserole, heat the beef stock and add, then simmer in the oven for about two to two and a half hours. Thicken the liquid as desired.

SAVOURY PIE

Ingredients

- 3 large cooked potatoes
- 6 tomatoes
- 1oz butter
- 3oz grated cheese
- milk
- seasoning

Method. Slice the potatoes, which may well be those left from a meal Peel and slice the tomatoes. Put a layer of potatoes at the bottom of a greased pie dish, season well. Put a layer of sliced tomato, season, then a layer of grated cheese. Repeat these layers till the dish is full, finishing with a layer of cheese. Put pats of butter on top and pour a little milk down the side. Put into a hot oven for the pie to heat through and for the cheese on top to brown.

SCALLOPED POTATOES AND HAM

Ingredients

- 1lb peeled sliced potatoes
- 1½ cups milk
- 2 teaspoons chopped onions
- 1 slice raw ham (gammon rasher)

Method. If ham is salt, soak in warm water for ½ hour, then drain and dry. Choose a slice ½ inch thick. Brown on both sides in a frying pan. Place in a deep fireproof baking dish. Cover with chopped onion and sliced potatoes, then with milk. Cover and bake in a slow oven for 1 hour. Uncover and bake another ½ hour.

BEEF PANCAKES

Ingredients

Pancakes:

4oz plain flour
good shake of white pepper
¼ pint milk
cooking fat or oil for frying
1 level teaspoon salt
2 eggs
3 tablespoons water

Pepperpot Filling and Sauce:

2oz butter or margarine
1 pint beef stock (or tomato juice)
1 teaspoon paprika
1 level teaspoon salt
12oz minced or chopped cooked beef or corned beef
2oz plain flour
2 tablespoons vinegar
1 teaspoon made mustard
¼ teaspoon black pepper (best freshly ground)

Method. Sift the flour and seasonings for the pancakes into a large bowl. Mix to a thick smooth batter with the beaten eggs and milk. Beat well until the bubbles rise to the top and then gently stir in the water. Leave, covered, in a cool place while preparing the filling.

Melt the 2oz fat in a pan and stir in the 2oz flour and cook, stirring, until lightly browned. Remove from heat and gradually stir in the stock. Heat, stirring, until the mixture boils and thickens. Simmer very gently 3 minutes. Stir in the vinegar, made mustard, paprika, pepper and salt. Add just enough sauce to the minced meat to moisten it; keep hot, reserving remaining sauce for serving.

Heat a little cooking fat or oil in a heavy frying pan, about 8in. across, until lightly smoking. Pour in sufficient batter to cover the base of pan thinly. Cook until underside is brown. Turn or toss and brown other side. Use up all batter in this way, piling the pancakes and keeping them hot in a kitchen towel.

Pile the hot filling in centre of the hot pancakes and quickly roll, or fold each one separately, and serve them piping hot. Grated cheese is usually served with them at the table. Reheat the remaining sauce, thinning to pouring consistency, and serve separately.

HOT-POT

Ingredients

1½lb potatoes
¼lb lean bacon
2oz butter
salt and pepper
1lb sheep's or lamb's liver
2 large onions
a little flour

Method. Peel potatoes thinly and cut into slices about ⅛ inch thick. Prepare and and slice liver, cut bacon into dice and slice onions. Melt butter in a frying pan, dip liver into a little flour and fry very gently with the bacon and onions. Transfer ingredients to a casserole, season well and cover with the potatoes. Bake in a moderately hot oven for 1½ to 2 hours. Remove lid of casserole for last ½ hour to brown potatoes.

BEEF BAKE

Ingredients

- $1\frac{1}{2}$lb stewing steak
- 1oz dripping
- 2 medium onions finely sliced
- 2 heaped teaspoons tomato puree
- 2oz white breadcrumbs
- 1oz flour, well seasoned with salt and pepper
- 1 pint water
- 2 carrots, sliced
- pinch mixed herbs
- $1\frac{1}{2}$oz butter

Topping:

- 8oz self-raising flour
- pepper
- 3 tablespoons cooking oil
- $\frac{1}{4}$ pint milk
- level teaspoon salt
- $\frac{1}{2}$ teaspoon dried onion powder (if liked)

Method. Cut meat into cubes. Toss cubes of meat in well seasoned flour. Melt dripping in a large frying pan or saucepan and gently fry onion until golden. Add the meat and fry a further 5 minutes turning until meat is brown. Remove from heat and blend in water and tomato puree. Add carrots and herbs. Return to heat and bring to the boil. Turn mixture into a 2 pint casserole. Cover with lid and cook in the middle of a medium oven for 2 hours.

Meanwhile fry breadcrumbs slowly in butter until golden brown. Then prepare topping. Sieve together flour, salt and pepper. Add the oil and milk and mix to a soft dough. Drop tablespoons of this dough into the buttered crumbs and roll into balls in the crumbs. Arrange on top of the stew. Return uncovered casserole to a fairly hot oven, for 40 minutes, until topping is golden brown.

POTATOES AND EGGS AU GRATIN

Ingredients

2lb cooked potatoes
2oz cooked chopped bacon or ham
1 pint milk
½ cup fresh breadcrumbs
2oz grated cheese
3 hard-boiled eggs
1oz butter or margarine
3 level tablespoons flour
salt and pepper to taste
½oz butter or margarine

Method. Slice the potatoes and eggs and put them in layers in a pie dish with the bacon. Melt 1oz butter and stir in the flour. Cook for 1 minute and add the milk, mix well until it boils and cook 1 minute. Season to taste. Pour over the potatoes. Melt the ½oz of butter and stir in the breadcrumbs, mixing until they are well coated. Combine crumbs and cheese and sprinkle over the top of the sauce. Bake in a moderate oven until brown on top and heated through, about 20 minutes.

HAM crusted with sugar

Method. Bake the ham in a slow oven, allowing 25 minutes per lb. An hour before cooked remove the rind and spread with the following crust:- One cup of brown sugar mixed with two tablespoons cider. Increase the heat for the last fifteen minutes to brown the ham. Baste with the drippings.

MEDLEY PIE

Method. Make enough slices of fat bacon to line a pie dish, cover with sliced onions and sprinkle over with one dessertspoon of sage. Add salt and pepper to taste. Cover with a good layer of apples, pared and quartered and sweeten to taste. Add half-a-teacup of water and cover the whole with a good short crust. Bake in a moderate oven until nicely brown.

CRUMBLE TOP BEEF PIE

Ingredients

1lb cooked beef, minced
½oz dripping
salt, pepper and nutmeg
1 onion
½ pint beef stock
2 teaspoons flour

Topping:

4oz plain flour
3oz Cheddar cheese, grated
2oz margarine
pinch salt

Method. Chop onion finely and fry in dripping until golden brown Add the flour to the pan and mix well to blend the flour with the surplus fat. Cook for two minutes, stirring so the flour browns but does not burn. Add stock and bring to the boil. Mix with minced meat, season with salt, pepper and nutmeg to taste and turn into a casserole.

To make the topping: Sift flour and add salt and rub in fat. Add grated cheese. Sprinkle the crumble mixture over the minced beef. Bake in a moderate oven for 30 to 40 minutes.

BUTTER BEAN HOT-POT

Ingredients

- 1lb butter beans (soaked overnight)
- 1 tablespoon syrup
- $\frac{3}{4}$pint boiling water
- 8oz bacon rashers
- 1oz demerara sugar
- 1 level teaspoon mustard

Method. Rinse the beans. Place in a casserole with the bacon. Mix sugar, syrup and mustard with the water. Pour over the beans. Cover and bake in a slow oven for about 3 hours.

POTATO PANCAKES

Method. Put a breakfast cup of cold mashed potatoes with 1 tablespoon flour. Add pepper and salt to season, $\frac{1}{4}$ teaspoon carbonate of soda and sufficient milk to make a batter. Beat well and then fry in a little hot fat until both sides are brown. Delicious served with bacon.

CHICKEN GOULASH (sent by a reader)

(Serves 4 to 6 persons)

Ingredients

- 1 fowl or roasting chicken
- 1$\frac{1}{2}$oz flour
- 2oz butter
- 12 button mushrooms
- forcemeat stuffing or sausage meat
- 12 small onions
- cream sauce

Method. Simmer giblets to make 1 pint of stock, stuff chicken with forcemeat or sausage meat. Brown the chicken in 2oz hot butter until golden brown, lift out and brown the onions. Lift out onions and stir flour into fat, cooking until golden brown, then add stock gradually, bring to the boil and cook for few minutes. If using a young chicken the onions can be put into the casserole with it — with a boiling fowl it is advisable to add them later in cooking period. Cover chicken with sauce, put lid on casserole. Allow 20 minutes per lb and 20 minutes over in a moderate oven; with an older boiling fowl allow 30 minutes for the lb and 30 minutes over in a moderate oven; add onions one hour before serving and mushrooms 30 minutes before serving for the cream sauce. Stir half cup of cream or top of the milk into the sauce in which chicken was cooked.

FARMHOUSE CHICKEN CASSEROLE

Ingredients

1lb potatoes
seasoned flour
4 rashers diced streaky bacon
6 button or spring onions
4 chicken joints
½oz butter
2oz quartered mushrooms
½ pint chicken stock

Method. Peel potatoes, cut in quarters or use small new potatoes, scraped. Toss chicken joints in seasoned flour. Melt the butter in a frying pan and fry chicken until golden brown. Place in a casserole dish with the potatoes. Fry bacon, onions and mushrooms until brown and add to the casserole. Add stock to the frying pan and stir until boiling. Pour into the casserole and cover. Bake in a moderate oven, for 1 hour or until tender. Sprinkle with chopped parsley and serve.

CHICKEN POTATO PIE

Ingredients

2oz margarine
1 pint chicken stock
the meat from half a cooked chicken, diced
4oz green peas
melted butter
2oz flour
¼ pint single cream
2oz cooked ham, diced
4oz mushrooms
creamed potatoes

Method. Heat margarine, blend in the flour and gradually add the chicken stock. Simmer until the mixture thickens slightly. Add cream, chicken, ham, mushrooms and peas and simmer for 15 minutes. Pour into a serving dish and decorate with piped mashed potatoes. Brush with melted butter and brown under a hot grill.

CHICKEN MINCE

Ingredients

1lb cooked chicken
stick celery
1oz flour
¼ pint milk
1 onion
1oz butter
½ breakfast-cup chicken stock

Method. Remove the meat from the bones and mince or dice finely. Finely chop onion and celery. Melt fat in a saucepan, stir in the flour and cook until quite smooth, but do not allow to colour. Gradually add the stock and milk, stirring constantly. Put in the celery and onion and simmer very gently for 15 minutes. Then put in the meat. Cover the pan and remove to a very slow oven for half an hour, the heat being sufficient only to allow the chicken to become flavoured, but not to cook further. Serve in a border of mashed potato.

HOT MEAT LOAF

Ingredients

- browned bread crumbs
- 1 medium onion, finely chopped and fried
- 2oz white breadcrumbs
- $\frac{1}{4}$ pint stock
- 8oz cooked meat, minced
- $\frac{1}{2}$ teaspoon mixed herbs
- $\frac{1}{2}$ teaspoon ground nutmeg
- 1 egg
- salt and pepper to season

Method. Grease a 1lb loaf tin and coat inside with browned bread-crumbs. Mix minced meat with chopped fried onion, herbs, bread-crumbs, beaten egg, stock and seasonings. Turn mixture in to prepared tin, cover with baking foil or greased paper and cook in a moderate oven for one hour. Turn out of tin and serve with tomato sauce made as follows:- skin 1lb tomatoes, finely chop them to a pulp. Gently heat in a saucepan with $\frac{1}{2}$ teaspoon brown sugar. Season well with salt and pepper. A little chopped parsley added just before serving makes this sauce delicious.

MUTTON HOT-POT

Ingredients

- one mutton chop per person
- a little flour
- seasoning
- a spoonful of brown sugar

For each chop allow:

- 1 large onion
- 2 large potatoes
- 2 carrots

Method. Flour and pepper chops, brown them in a little fat in a frying pan. Pack into a tall casserole or deep saucepan. Chop the vegetables except the potatoes, and fry them adding to the meat afterwards. Cut the potatoes into thick slices, and cover the top of the pan closely with them adding seasoning as you do so. Add a spoonful of flour to the fat in which you have fried the vegetables, let it cook, then add water until you have a good thick gravy, adding the sugar at the last moment. Pour this over the meat and potatoes, put on the lid and cook for 2 hours. Just before cooking is completed remove the lid and let the potatoes brown.

MUTTON PUDDING

Ingredients

- 2lb mutton, without bone
- 1 sheep's kidney, with fat
- about 8oz flour
- 1 onion
- seasoning and herbs
- parsley if available

Method. Remove the fat from the kidney, chop it finely, and make a good suet crust with the fat and the flour, adding herbs and plenty of seasoning. Chop the meat and kidney into small cubes, add the chopped parsley, the onion, a little flour and plenty of seasoning.

Line a greased bowl with the suet crust, pack the meat mixture into it, add stock, and put on a suet lid. Boil for two hours or steam for three.

Country women would add to this, in summer, thyme flowers and leaves, in autumn, rowan berries, in winter pickled damsons.

—J. A. Teats

Herding Sheep at Warcop

STUFFED LOIN OF PORK

Ingredients

3lb loin of pork
4oz breadcrumbs
1oz butter
4 large onions
1 teaspoon crushed herbs
seasoning to taste

Method. Boil the onions, drain and chop finely. Mix with breadcrumbs, herbs, butter and seasoning. Cut a pocket in the meat and fill with the stuffing. Put in a roasing tin and bake in a moderate oven for 2 hours.

LAMB CASTLES

Little hot topsy-turvy puddings to serve with green vegetables.

Ingredients

Lamb mixture:
8oz cooked lean lamb finely minced
seasoning to taste
2oz soft breadcrumbs
3 to 4 tablespoons tomato ketchup

Pudding mixture:
6oz self-raising flour
liberal sprinkle white pepper
$\frac{1}{4}$level teaspoon dried rosemary or thyme
$\frac{1}{2}$ level teaspoon salt
2oz margarine or cooking fat
1 medium egg, lightly beaten
6 to 7 tablespoons milk or water to mix

Method. Mix together lamb and breadcrumbs, bind with tomato ketchup. Season to taste. Divide equally between 6 well-greased castle pudding moulds or individual pudding basins. Sift flour, salt and pepper into a bowl. Rub in fat, add herbs, mix to adropping consistency with the beaten egg and milk. Three-quarters fill the small basins with the mixture then cover with greaseproof paper or aluminium foil. Steam steadily for about 30 minutes.

CREAMED KIDNEYS

Ingredients

6 lambs' kidney
1oz flour
salt and pepper to season
bacon rolls and parsley to garnish
2oz butter
$\frac{1}{2}$ pint milk
3 tablespoons dairy cream

Method. Skin and slice the kidneys and fry gently in the butter for five minutes. Remove from pan. Add the flour to the pan and cook gently for 1 minute. Remove from heat and gradually stir in the milk. Season and bring to the boil, stirring constantly; add the kidneys and cook for a further three minutes. Cool slightly then stir in the cream. Garnish with bacon rolls and chopped parsley. Delicious with toast.

SAVOURY APPLE AND BACON PUDDING

Ingredients

Suet Pastry:

8oz self-raising flour
½ level teaspoon dry mustard
about ¼ pint cold water
1 level teaspoon salt
4oz suet, finely chopped

Filling:

1lb streaky bacon, roughly chopped
½lb cooking apples, peeled, cored and diced
4oz cabbage heart, chopped fine
1 large onion, chopped fine
2 level tablespoons black treacle
pepper to taste

Method. Mix all filling ingredients together. Into another bowl sift flour and salt together. Add suet and toss all together. Mix to stiff dough with the water. Roll out two-thirds of dough to line 2½ pint well greased pudding basin. Fill with bacon and vegetable mixture and cover with lid made by rolling out the rest of the dough. Cover with greased greaseproof paper and steam steadily for 3 hours.

STUFFED MEAT ROLLS

Ingredients

1½lb silverside, cut into 6 slices
6 rashers back bacon

Stuffing:

2 large onions, finely chopped
1 tablespoon oil
2oz cheese, grated
1oz sultanas
1 teaspoon salt
2oz butter
6oz fresh white breadcrumbs
1 level teaspoon marjoram
1oz blanched almonds, chopped
pepper

For braising:

1 tablespoon oil
½ pint stock or water
3 tablespoons tomato puree
salt and pepper

Method. Trim off any excess fat from meat. Lay on a board and flatten with a rolling pin until very thin. Fry bacon gently for 1 minute on each side then place a rasher on each slice of meat.

Stuffing: Cook onions gently in butter and oil without browning for 3 to 4 minutes. Remove half the onions and keep on one side. Add rest of stuffing ingredients to remaining onions and mix well. Divide equally between meat slices and press down. Roll up tightly and secure ends with cocktail sticks.

To braise: Heat oil in a large flame-proof casserole or frying pan. Brown meat rolls evenly on all sides. Add remaining onion and tomato puree mixed with stock or water, season and bring to the boil. If cooked in a frying pan place meat and sauce in a large casserole. Bake in a low oven for 45 minutes until meat is tender.

FAMILY PICNIC PASTY

Ingredients

Shortcrust Pastry:

12oz self-raising flour
6oz lard
1 level teaspoon salt
4 to 5 tablespoons cold water to mix

Filling:

1 large onion, boiled and coarsely chopped
3 to 4 tablespoons cooked peas or runner beans
½ level teaspoon dry mustard
seasoning to taste
1 each, large potato and carrot, cooked and diced
6 to 8oz cold cooked beef or lamb, or corned beef, coarsely chopped

Method. Sift dry ingredients into bowl. Rub in fats till mixture resembles fine breadcrumbs. Mix to stiff paste with cold water. Turn out on to floured board, knead lightly till smooth, then divide in two. Roll each half into a rectangle, approximately 10in by 12in. Put one piece of rolled pastry on to greased baking sheet and cover with filling ingredients to within 1in of edges. Season to taste. Moisten edges with water then cover with remaining pastry. Press edges together to seal, trim for neatness then "ridge" with a fork. Brush top with beaten egg or milk, then decorate with pastry leaves, rolled and cut from trimmings. Bake at centre of moderate oven, 35 to 40 minutes.

SUMMER PATE LOAF

Ingredients

1 white plain loaf
4oz streaky bacon
¾lb pig's liver
¼ teaspoon garlic powder (optional)
pepper
oil for brushing
1 tablespoon oil
1 large onion, finely chopped
1 egg, beaten
½ teaspoon fine herbs
1 teaspoon salt
2 eggs, hard boiled

Method. Cut a horizontal slice across top of loaf and scoop out the inside. Use 4oz of this to make breadcrumbs. Cut bacon into ¼in pieces and fry gently for 3 to 4 minutes until crisp. Remove then cook onion gently for 3 to 4 minutes. Add to bacon. Chop liver very finely. Cook quickly in remaining oil for 3 to 4 minutes stirring continuously. Add to bacon and onions with breadcrumbs, beaten egg, garlic and herbs. Mix thoroughly together.

Press half the mixture into bottom of loaf. Place whole hard boiled eggs in a line down the centre and cover with remaining mixture, being careful not to move eggs. Cover with top of loaf and wrap tightly in foil. Bake in a moderate oven for 1¼ hours. At the end of this time remove foil and brush bread with oil, continue baking for $\frac{1}{4}$ hour. Leave to cool. Cut into 8 slices with a sharp knife and re-assemble to shape of loaf.

7. Fish Dishes

POTTED CHAR
(the Char is a Windermere fish)

Method. Clean and scale the fish and cook it slowly in white wine with a few slices of onion and carrot and pieces of parsley stalk. Allow to cool, skin it, and remove the fillets. Be careful to take out all bones. Now arrange the fillets or pieces of fillet in an earthenware pot and cover them with melted butter. Place the pot, with contents covered, in a moderate oven for 20 to 30 minutes, and on withdrawing add more clarified butter if required. (Fillets must be covered with butter). Will keep for some time in a cool place.

CRUMBLE TOPPED FISH PIE

Ingredients

- 4oz onion, peeled and finely chopped
- 2 level teaspoons dried mustard
- 1 dessertspoon lemon juice or 1 teaspoon vinegar
- 3 standard eggs, hard boiled and coarsely chopped
- 2oz butter or margarine
- 2oz plain flour
- $\frac{3}{4}$ pint milk
- $1\frac{1}{2}$lb smoked haddock, cooked skinned and finely flaked
- seasoning to taste

Method. Gently fry the onion in the fat till pale gold. Stir in flour and mustard and cook 2 minutes. Remove from heat, and very gradually add milk. Cook, stirring till sauce comes to the boil and thickens. Simmer 3 minutes. Stir in lemon juice or vinegar, eggs and flaked fish. Season to taste and transfer mixture to a large shallow oven-proof dish.

Crumble Topping:

- 4oz plain flour
- good shake of pepper
- 2 to 3 oz Cheddar cheese, finely grated
- large pinch of salt
- 2 oz butter or margarine

Method. Sift flour and seasoning together. Rub in fat finely, add cheese and toss lightly together to mix. Sprinkle topping thickly over fish mixture then re-heat towards the top of a moderate oven for 30 to 40 minutes, or until crumble is a rich gold.

FISHY PIE

Ingredients

Filling:
1lb smoked haddock
½ pint milk
1oz butter
1oz flour
2 hard boiled eggs, coarsely chopped
1 tablespoon parsley, chopped
pepper

Pastry:
12oz plain flour
½ teaspoon salt
3oz margarine
3oz lard
about 3 tablespoons water
milk or beaten egg for glazing

Method.

Filling: Poach haddock in a little of the milk, cool slightly. Remove bones and skin then flake. Melt butter in a pan, add flour and cook a minute without browning. Make fish liquor up to ½ pint with milk. Remove pan from heat and gradually add milk, return to heat, bring to the boil, stirring until thickened. Remove from heat and stir in haddock, eggs, parsley and pepper. Cool.

Pastry Fish: Sift together flour and salt, rub in margarine and lard until mixture resembles fine breadcrumbs. Mix together with water to form a firm dough. Divide pastry in half and roll out both pieces to 2 oblongs, about 12in. by 8in., and just under ¼in. thick. Cut out using a 12in. oval serving plate as a guide. Press an upturned wire cooling rack on to one piece of pastry to make a criss-cross impression on the pastry to resemble scales, shape the mouth and tail on both pastry ovals. Lift the plain pastry fish onto a baking sheet, spread with fish mixture to within 1in. of edge. Brush edges with milk or egg. Cover with pastry fish, scale side up, and seal edges. Using a fork make marks like fins round the edge. Form an eye with the pastry trimmings. Brush whole fish with milk or egg. Bake in a hot oven for about 20 minutes, then lower to medium for a further 20 minutes.

FISH PIE

Ingredients

1lb cod or haddock, etc.
cold mashed potatoes
a little cheese (grated) and breadcrumbs

Parsley sauce:
¾ pint milk
1 dessertspoon cornflour
finely chopped parsley
2oz butter
pepper and salt

Method. Boil the fish, remove skin and bones, and flake. Make the parsley sauce and pour over the fish. Cover with mashed potatoes and sprinkle the top with breadcrumbs and grated cheese. Bake in a moderate oven till nicely browned.

CREAMED FISH WITH POTATO BORDER

Ingredients

1lb cooked sieved potatoes
1lb fresh haddock
½ oz butter
¾ pint white sauce
2 eggs
2oz grated cheese

Method. Steam and mash the potatoes. Add eggs and butter. Beat and season to taste. Shape with floured hands into a round border in a buttered fireproof dish and ornament with a fork. Bake in a moderate oven until brown. Meanwhile, boil, drain and flake haddock into white sauce. Stir in grated cheese. Season to taste. Stir till cheese is melted. Pour into the border. Sprinkle fish with chopped parsley.

SCALLOPED FISH

Ingredients

2 cups sieved, boiled or steamed potato
2 cups steamed white fish
1½ cups well-seasoned white sauce
½ cup stale crumbs
1 tablespoon chopped chives
2 tablespoons melted butter
pepper and salt to taste
paprika to taste

Method. Add paprika, chives and pepper and salt to taste to the potato. Line a shallow buttered fireproof dish thinly with the mixture. Add a layer of flaked fish, then half the sauce. Cover with remainder of potato, then with remainder of sauce. Sprinkle with crumbs, then with butter. Bake in a moderate oven for 25 minutes.

SALMON KEDGEREE

Ingredients

3oz long grain rice
1oz butter
1 tomato
8oz tin of red salmon
2oz grated Cheddar cheese
¼ pint cream, whipped

Method. Cook rice in boiling salted water for 15 minutes, drain well. Melt butter in frying pan, mix in the rice and flaked salmon, season and fold in the whipped cream. Place in an oven-proof dish, sprinkle with grated cheese and decorate with sliced tomato. Place in a hot oven for 8 to 10 minutes until cheese topping is melted.

—Derek Widdicombe

Early morning reflections in Derwentwater

8. Jams, Jellies and Preserves

HAW JELLY

Ingredients

3lb of haws
granulated sugar
3 pints water
lemons

Method. Wash the haws and put into a pan with the water; allow to simmer for one hour, pour into a jelly bag and leave to strain overnight. Next day measure the juice and return to the pan with 1lb granulated sugar and the juice of one lemon to each pint of juice. Boil until the jelly will set when tested.

REDCURRANT JELLY

Ingredients

2lb redcurrants
½ pint water
granulated sugar

Method. Wash the currants (there is no need to remove the stalks) and put into a preserving pan with the water; simmer gently until the currants are tender. Strain through a jelly bag. Allow 14oz sugar to each pint of juice. Return juice to preserving pan and stir in the sugar. Bring slowly to the boil and boil fairly fast until a little of the mixture will jell on a plate when tested. Put into warmed jars. Cover when quite cold.

APPLE GINGER

Ingredients

2lb apples
4oz crystallized ginger (shredded)
2lb loaf sugar
1½ pints water

Method. Boil sugar and water to a syrup. Peel, core and cut apples in quarters (dip in cold water to preserve colour). Add ginger and syrup, boil until transparent. Put in jars and store in a dry place.

CUMBERLAND RHUBARB JAM

Method. To each lb of rhubarb add 1lb sugar. Cut rhubarb into fine dice, place in enamel bowl along with sugar, allow to stand overnight. Then pour off the syrup into enamel pan and just bring to the boil. Pour the hot juice on the cut rhubarb and repeat the process by pouring the juice into pan and bringing to the boil again. Repeat 3 times then boil the rhubarb and juice with the juice of 2 lemons together until the jam sets. Pour into warm jars and cover.

DAMSON JAM

Ingredients

4lb damsons
4lb granulated sugar
a good half-pint water

Method. Wash the damsons and allow to dry, then simmer them gently in the water until soft, remove the stones as they come to the top. Add the sugar which has been warmed in the oven, stir to dissolve it and bring to the boil. Boil moderately fast until a little will set when tested. Put into warmed jars and cover when cold.

BILBERRY JAM

Ingredients

2lb bilberries
2lb sugar
1 tablespoon boiling water

Method. Put all ingredients into a suitable pan. Bring to the boil and boil rapidly for 15 minutes. Pour the jam out of the pan into warm jars. Do not scrape it out, as a great number of small seeds adhere to the pan sides, and the jam is best without them.

LEMON BUTTER

Ingredients

1oz butter
1½ cups demerara sugar
3 eggs
grated rind and juice of 2 lemons

Method. Place butter in a double boiler over steaming water and allow to melt, add the lightly beaten eggs, sugar, lemon rind and juice and stir all together, then stir occasionally until mixture thickens.

LEMON CHEESE

Ingredients

¼lb butter
2 eggs
1 cup sugar
juice and rind of two lemons

Method. Put butter and sugar in pan and melt, stir in juice and grated rind of lemons, add gently the well-beaten eggs, stir till it thickens. DO NOT BOIL. Put into jars and cover.

BLACKCURRANT SYRUP

Method. Wash the blackcurrants and put into a pan (stainless steel, aluminium or enamel). Do not add any more water than adheres to the fruit after washing. Bring to the boil, stirring con-

—J. P. Delaney

Shepherd near Watendlath

stantly and boil for two minutes only. Strain the fruit through a jelly bag, overnight. Next day add 12oz granulated sugar to each pint of juice and stir until the sugar dissolves. Pour into screw-top bottles to within 2 inches of the top and seal. Sterilise by placing the bottles in a pan with a false bottom (slats of wood or newspaper placed in the bottom of an ordinary pan will serve quite well) and fill the pan with water up to the base of the screw cap. Heat to 170 degrees Far. and maintain for 20 minutes without boiling. Cool the bottles and store in a cool, dark place.

GOOSEBERRY MARMALADE

Ingredients

2lb gooseberries
3lb granulated sugar
2 pints water
juice and grated rind of 1 lemon

Method. Top and tail the gooseberries and place in a preserving pan with the rest of the ingredients. Bring to the boil and continue boiling for 1¼ hours or until set, test for setting by placing a very small quantity on a saucer and cooling; if a skin forms on top the preserve is cooked. Put into warm jars and cover when cold.

SEVILLE ORANGE MARMALADE

Ingredients

1lb seville oranges
1½lb sugar to each lb of boiled fruit
3 pints water and juice

Method. Choose thick-skinned oranges, wash and cut in half, squeezing out the juice and put with pips into a basin. Slice the peel finely (or mince), add the water and the pips in a muslin bag. Leave to stand overnight or boil at once until the peel is tender when cut with a spoon. Now weigh carefully and add 1½lb preserving sugar to each lb of boiled fruit. Heat slowly and then boil very fast for 30 minutes and test for set. Leave to stand a few minutes, then fill warm jars and seal.

MINCEMEAT

Ingredients

1lb sweet apples
1lb currants
½lb butter
1lb stoned raisins
1lb Scotch moist sugar
1 teaspoon ground cinnamon

Method. Peel the apples and cut into quarters, clean the raisins and currants and put all through a fine mincer, add sugar and cinnamon and mix in, melt the butter and add this, stirring well in.

MARROW PICKLE

1lb marrow cut up into square pieces. Put into a bowl and sprinkle with salt. Leave overnight and strain next morning.

The pickle:

½lb sugar
1½oz dry mustard
6 chillies
2 pints vinegar
1½oz ground ginger
½oz tumeric
4 cloves

Boil these together for 10 minutes, stirring all the time, then add the marrow cubes and boil till tender. Put into warm jars and cover when cold.

TOMATO CHUTNEY

Ingredients

¾lb sultanas
1lb cooking apples
½lb soft brown sugar
¼ teaspoon pepper
2lb green tomatoes
½lb onions
¼ teaspoon salt
¼ teaspoon dry mustard

Method. Remove the skin from onions, core the apples but do not peel. Then put all the ingredients through the mincer, put into a saucepan or preserving pan, boil until stiff and bottle when cool.

PICKLED PLUMS

Ingredients

4lb plums
¼oz cinnamon
2 pints vinegar
3lb white sugar
¼oz cloves

Method. Pick the plums and wipe them. Put the vinegar into a suitable pan and drop the plums in. Put over heat and when hot add the sugar. Bring to the boil and continue to boil gently until the plums are tender. Put into warmed jars and cover.

PICKLED ONIONS

Ingredients

6lb shallots
2 cups boiled vinegar
¾lb soft brown sugar
salt
1oz pickling spice
2 wine-glasses sherry

Method. Peel shallots and cover with salt, leave for 24 hours. Boil the vinegar and allow to cool then mix in the sugar and sherry. Fill jars with the onions, pour over the pickle. Leave for three weeks before using.

PICKLED ONIONS WITH SHERRY

Ingredients

6lb shallots
2 cups boiled vinegar
¾lb demerara sugar
1oz pickling spice
2 wine glasses sherry
salt

Method. Peel shallots and cover with salt, leave for 24 hours. Boil the vinegar and allow to cool, then mix in the sugar and sherry and stir until sugar is dissolved. Fill jars with the onions, pour over the vinegar pickle and seal. Leave for three to four weeks before using.

PICCALILLI

Ingredients

1lb onions
1lb green tomatoes
salt
1lb cucumber
1 medium sized cauliflower

Method. Clean vegetables and cut into suitably sized pieces. Cook in well salted water until tender. Then strain off the water and pour into the boiled dressing, stir well and cook for 5 minutes.

Dressing:

$\frac{3}{4}$ cup sugar
$\frac{1}{4}$oz tumeric
$1\frac{1}{2}$ pints vinegar
1 dessertspoon dry mustard
$\frac{3}{4}$ cup flour

Method. Mix the dry ingredients well together and mix with a little of the cold vinegar. Boil the rest of the vinegar and stir in the mixture. Pour over the vegetables and stir well, then boil all for about five minutes.

9. Trimmings and Toffee

CUMBERLAND SAUCE

Ingredients

4 level tablespoons redcurrant jelly
1 level teaspoon made mustard
2 tablespoons port wine or elderberry wine
rind of 1 lemon finely sliced and boiled until tender

Method. Mix well together the redcurrant jelly, wine and mustard, add the cooked lemon rind and stir in. May be served hot or cold.

CLEAR LEMON SAUCE

Ingredients

1 pint water
2 tablespoons sugar
2 tablespoons cornflour
1 lemon

Method. Put water on to boil, then add cornflour and sugar mixed to a paste with cold water, mix in grated rind and juice of lemon and boil for five minutes. Serve hot.

SALAD DRESSING

Ingredients

1 teaspoon dry mustard
1 egg
1 dessertspoon sugar
½ teaspoon salt
1 dessertspoon butter
½ cup milk
2 dessertspoons vinegar

Method. Mix mustard, salt and sugar in a basin, add the egg, stir well and add the milk. Stand the basin in a saucepan of boiling water over the heat, put in the butter and stir until butter is melted. Remove from heat, add vinegar, return to boiling water and cook carefully, stirring continually until the mixture thickens.

CAKE FILLING

Ingredients

1 banana
1 dessertspoon raspberry jam
1 tablespoon cream

Method. Mash the banana, mix in the jam and cream.

MARSHMALLOW ICING

Method. Boil together for 5 minutes, but do not stir, 1 cup water, 1 cup sugar, 1 tablespoon gelatine. Leave till cold, then whisk until like cream. Pour over cake and down the sides. Sprinkle with coconut, chopped nuts or grated chocolate. Do not beat too stiff as this mixture sets very quickly when turned on to the cake.

MOCK CREAM

Ingredients

- Half a cup of milk
- 1 tablespoon butter
- vanilla essence to taste
- 1 dessertspoon cornflour
- 1 tablespoon sugar

Method. Beat to a cream the butter and sugar. Mix the cornflour with a little of the milk, boil the rest of the milk and stir into the cornflour, then return to pan and boil for one minute. Allow to cool. Add to the creamed butter and sugar, flavour with vanilla essence.

TREACLE TOFFEE

Ingredients

- 1lb Scotch moist sugar
- 4oz treacle
- 1 tablespoon water
- 4oz butter
- 1 tablespoon vinegar
- 1 tablespoon milk

Method. Bring all ingredients except vinegar to the boil, stirring all the time. Boil gently for about twenty minutes, stirring all the time, until the mixture goes brittle when a little is dropped into cold water. Stir in the vinegar and pour into well greased shallow tins. Score into conveniently sized pieces with a sharp knife when nearly set.

FUDGE

Ingredients

- 1lb soft brown sugar
- 1 cup chopped walnuts
- a piece of butter the size of a walnut

Method. Put all the ingredients into a saucepan over low heat and stir until the sugar has dissolved, bring slowly to the boil and boil for three minutes, stirring gently all the time. Remove from heat and beat until the mixture is thick. Pour into tins previously greased with butter and cut into squares when cold.

AMBLESIDE TOFFEE

Ingredients

2lb white sugar

$\frac{1}{2}$ a large tin condensed milk

a pinch of salt

$\frac{1}{4}$lb butter

1 teacup water

Method. Put all ingredients in a strong pan, stir over gentle heat, taking care it does not burn. When toffee begins to thicken, take off heat and stir for one minute, add a few drops of vanilla essence. Pour into a well-buttered tin and when cold mark off into squares.

10. Rum Butter

Here are three recipes:

Ingredients

1lb castor sugar
½lb butter
a little grated nutmeg
wineglass rum

Method. Beat butter to cream, and add sugar and nutmeg. Beat well until quite smooth and mixture will drop off spoon. Add rum and mix well. Put into bowl and allow to set.

Ingredients

½lb butter
½lb brown sugar (soft)
three tablespoons rum

Method. Melt butter. Do not let it boil but "just soften" it, and beat in sugar. Stir in rum, a tablespoon at a time. Put the mixture into your best bowl and use when set.

Ingredients

1lb brown sugar
½lb butter
1 wineglass rum
half nutmeg

Method. Mix sugar, nutmeg and rum. Melt butter and pour over sugar, etc., and stir well.